The Great Outdoors

Look for these
Road to Writing
books

Mile 4 • First Journals

The Great Outdoors
Me, Myself, and I

Mile 5 • Journals

Best Friends
Imagine That!

In This Book
You Can:

- Write your own stories.

- Illustrate your ideas.

- Brainstorm silly topics.

- Be creative!

A GOLDEN BOOK · New York
Golden Books Publishing Company, Inc. New York, New York 10106

ISBN: 0-307-45450-9   A MM

The Great Outdoors

by Sarah Albee
illustrated by Gerald Kelley

BRAINSTORM!

Things I like to do outdoors:

1._____

2._____

3._____

4._____

5._____

Pick one.
Why do you like
to do it?

_____

_____

_____

_____

_____

_____

_____

_____

BRAINSTORM!

Things I don't like to do outdoors:

1._____

2._____

3._____

4._____

5._____

Pick one.
Why don't you like to do it?

_____

_____

_____

_____

_____

Write a letter.
Explain why you're the best person for this job.

HELP WANTED:
Zookeeper's Assistant
Must like snakes,
cleaning cages, and
skunks.
If interested please write to
Ms. R.U. Kraysie.

Date:_____

Dear Ms. Kraysie:

_____

_____

_____

_____

_____

_____

_____

Sincerely yours,

_____

Things I need to pack
for a visit to the rain forest:

PACKING LIST

_____

_____

_____

_____

_____

_____

_____

Things I need to pack
for a visit to the desert:

PACKING LIST

_____

_____

_____

_____

_____

_____

_____

What's your favorite season?

_____

What are the best things about it?

_____

_____

_____

_____

_____

_____

What's your least favorite season?

_____

What are the worst things about it?

_____

_____

_____

_____

_____

_____

Write down the words you think of when you look at the stars.

_____

_____

_____

_____

_____

Write a poem about stars.

_____

_____

_____

_____

_____

_____

_____

_____

_____

_____

_____

_____

_____

_____

Explain to this Martian how to pack
a picnic basket.

First, _____

_____

_____

_____

Then, _____

_____

_____

_____

Next, _____

_____

_____

_____

Finally, _____

_____

_____

_____

Choose one chore
you have to do outdoors.
Invent something
that will make it
easier to do.

Describe your invention.

_____

_____

_____

_____

_____

_____

_____

Draw it.

BRAINSTORM!

Things I do to cool off:

1._____

2._____

3._____

4._____

5._____

Pick one.
How do you do it?

_____

_____

_____

_____

_____

_____

_____

_____

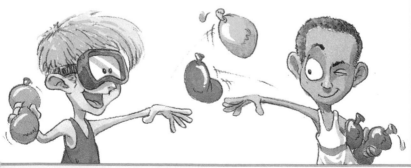

Make a list of the states
you've visited.

_____

_____

_____

_____

_____

_____

_____

Pick one.
Write about your trip.

My Trip to

_____

By

_____

_____

_____

_____

_____

_____

_____

You're stranded
on a desert island.

Let's see,
scrambled coconut
or fried coconut?

How did you get there?

_____

_____

_____

_____

How will you get off the island?

_____

_____

_____

_____

Draw yourself on the island.

Think of words that describe the
sounds these things make:

a cricket

_____

_____

_____

thunder

_____

_____

_____

wind

_____

_____

_____

a bird

_____

_____

_____

You have a job selling sand.
What are three uses for your sand?

1._____

2._____

3._____

List three reasons why your sand is
the best.

1._____

2._____

3._____

Design an ad for your sand.
Draw your ad here.

Tennis, anyone?

What are your three favorite outdoor sports? Write about them.

1. _____

_____

_____

_____

2. _____

_____

_____

_____

3. _____

_____

_____

_____

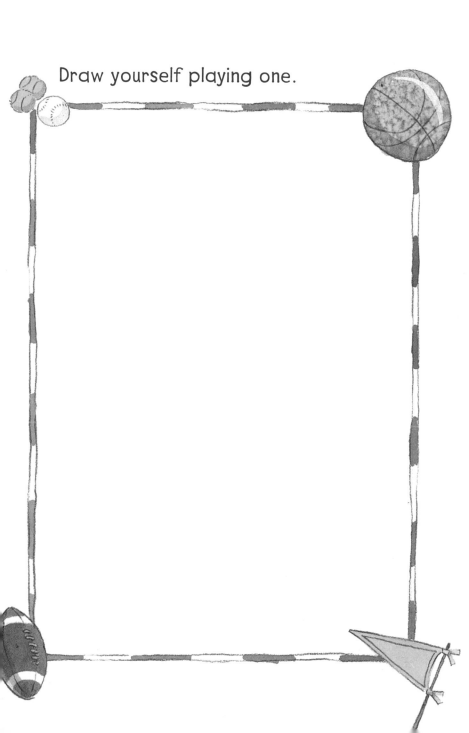

Draw yourself playing one.

Fill in the words.
(Don't peek at the following page!)

1._____
(something you wear on your feet)

2._____
(a word to describe something)

3._____
(an action word)

4._____
(a word to describe something)

5._____
(a piece of clothing)

6._____
(a word to describe something)

Finish this weather report.

The weather today will be

_____
(#4)

and _____ .
(#2)

Be sure to wear your

_____
(#5)

and _____ .
(#1)

Be careful if you

_____ .
(#3)

Tomorrow should be

_____ .
(#6)

You're a polar bear.
Describe a day in your life.

This morning I _____

_____

_____

_____

_____

_____

_____

_____

_____

And then I went to bed.

Draw a picture of your den.

BRAINSTORM!

Things I like to do at the beach:

1._____

2._____

3._____

4._____

5._____

Pick one.
Write about it.

_____

_____

_____

_____

_____

_____

_____

_____

_____

Imagine you are holding a balloon
and you let it go.
Write about your balloon's journey.

First, _____

_____

_____

_____

_____

Then, _____

_____

_____

_____

_____

Next, _____

_____

_____

_____

_____

Finally, _____

_____

_____

_____

_____

Describe your fantasy camping trip.

_____

_____

_____

_____

_____

_____

_____

_____

_____

Draw a picture of your campsite.

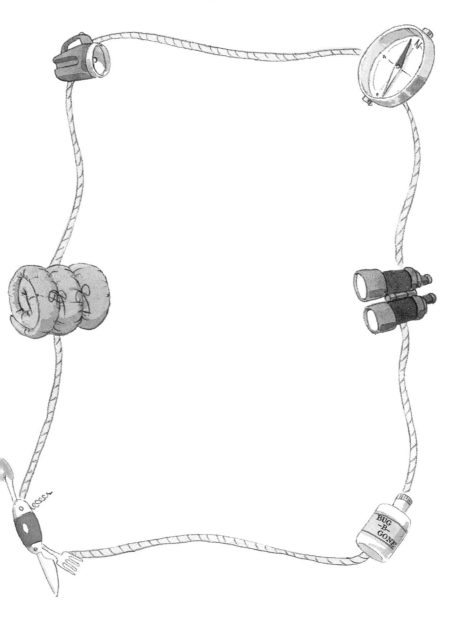

BRAINSTORM!

Things I like to do in the snow.

1._____

2._____

3._____

4._____

5._____

Pick one.
Write about it.

_____

_____

_____

_____

_____

_____

_____

Write a letter.
Explain why you're the best person for this job.

HELP WANTED:
Yard work, moat cleaning, hedge clipping, and animal care.
Interested workers please write to Sir L.

Date:_____

Dear Sir L.:

_____

_____

_____

_____

_____

_____

_____

_____

Sincerely yours,

_____

Write down the words you think of when it rains.

_____

_____

_____

_____

_____

_____

_____

Write a poem about rain.

_____

_____

_____

_____

_____

_____

_____

_____

_____

_____

You're making a time capsule
to take to the moon.
What will you put
in it from your house?

_____

_____

_____

_____

_____

_____

What will you put
in it from your school?

_____

_____

_____

_____

_____

_____

_____

You're an eagle.
Describe a day in your life.

This morning I _____

_____

_____

_____

_____

_____

_____

_____

_____

And then I went to bed.

Draw what you see from your nest.

Bugs that bug me:

1._____

2._____

3._____

4._____

Why?

_____

_____

_____

_____

_____

_____

Bugs I like:

1._____

2._____

3._____

4._____

Why?

_____

_____

_____

_____

_____

_____

Write down the words you think of
when you look out your window.

_____

_____

_____

_____

_____

_____

_____

Write a poem about what you see.

Write a letter.
Explain why you're the best person for this job.

Date:_____

Dear Mr. Rogers:

_____

_____

_____

_____

_____

_____

_____

_____

Sincerely yours,

_____

Ask someone you know:

1. What is your favorite thing to do outside?

_____

_____

_____

_____

2. Why do you like to do it?

_____

_____

_____

_____

Make up your own questions.

Ask someone you know to answer them.

3._____

_____

_____

_____

_____

4._____

_____

_____

_____

_____

_____

Use the answers you just got
to write a story.

_____

_____

_____

_____

_____

_____

_____

_____

_____

_____

Draw a picture to illustrate your story.

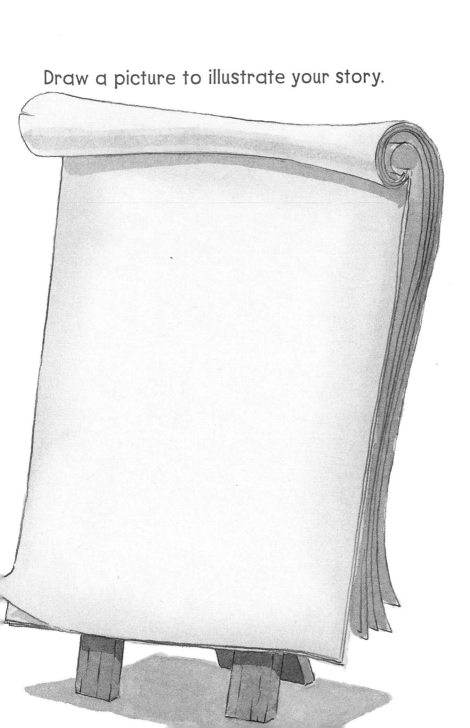

Imagine you are sitting on a cloud.
Write what you see below.

I see:

_____

_____

_____

_____

_____

_____

_____

_____